PHILIPPIANS
A SELF-STUDY GUIDE

D1523890

Irving L. Jensen

MOODY PRESS
CHICAGO

© 1973 by
THE MOODY BIBLE INSTITUTE
OF CHICAGO

Scripture quotations, unless noted otherwise, are from the King James Version.

The use of selected references from various versions of the Bible in this publication does not necessarily imply publisher endorsement of the version in its entirety.

Cover photo: The Arch of Galleries at Thessalonica, Greece

ISBN: 0-8024-4474-1

3 5 7 9 10 8 6 4 2

Printed in the United States of America

Contents

Introduction

There is something warm and personal about a friendly letter from one person to another or from one person to a group. We can well understand why God chose this form of writing to make up one-third of the New Testament. "Under the law, prophets delivered *oracles* to the *people*, solemnly setting forth their authoritative pronouncements with a 'thus saith the Lord.' With the inauguration of the age of grace, the apostles wrote *letters* to the *brethren* in a spirit of loving intimacy, setting forth the significance and implications of their new position in Christ."[1] One continual reminder to us as we read the New Testament epistles is that Christianity is personal; it involves the thoughts and actions of individual believers every day of their lives.

Doctrine and practice are the two main areas of a New Testament epistle. The doctrines give us the divinely inspired interpretations of the facts of the gospel, and the practical sections give us the reasonable demands and natural fruits of that gospel in the lives of the children of God.

Your study of Philippians can be a fruitful experience. Remember, Paul's letter is God's Word to *you*. Let it fulfill God's design. It is profitable for teaching, reproof, correction, and training in righteousness: that you may be well prepared and adequately equipped for every good work (see 2 Tim. 3:16-17).

Suggestions for Study

1. Spend most of your time studying the words and phrases of the Bible text. It is more effective when you see for yourself what the Bible says than when you hear or read about it second-hand. Remember that God intended the Bible to be read and stud-

---

1. D. Edmond Heibert, *An Introduction to the Pauline Epistles*, p. 14.

4

ied by everyone, not just the scholar. This manual is an aid for your study, not a substitute for it.

2. Train your eyes to see what the text actually says. When a verse is familiar because of earlier associations, it is easy to overlook an important word or phrase. A good Bible edition with large print and wide margins will enhance your study immeasurably. You will never regret an investment of money here.

3. Have a pencil in hand whenever you study. Mark your Bible freely. For example, mark where each new paragraph begins so that you are aware of paragraph context as you study. Underlining strong words and phrases is a must. Write out answers in the study manual. Record as many observations as you can on the analytical charts that appear in some of the lessons.

4. Always let the Bible speak for itself. The immediate context of a verse is usually its best interpreter.

5. Meditation and contemplation are important exercises in Bible study. Look upward; look within; look around. Always aim at applying the Bible passage to your own life in your relations to God and to man.

Study Steps

Most of the lessons in this book contain six main parts:

1. *Preparation for study.* These preliminary studies will help set the stage for your analysis by providing background and review to get you started in the right direction.

2. *Analysis.* This is the heart of all Bible study. Many questions are included in each lesson. Also worksheets (e.g., analytical charts) for recording observations and survey charts for views of context, appear throughout the manual.

3. *Notes.* The comments made here are usually about words and phrases whose meanings and background are not fully given by the immediate context.

4. *For thought and discussion.* This part of the lesson stresses application of the Bible text and will be of special interest if you are studying in a group.

5. *Further study.* Related subjects for extended study are identified here. Continuity in the lessons does not depend on your completing this phase.

6. *Words to ponder.* The concluding note is offered to encourage you to reflect upon the Bible text you have just studied.

1. Determine how much of each lesson may be adequately studied at each group meeting. Assign homework accordingly. Remind your group to write out answers to all questions.

2. Start the meeting on time; close on time. Extended discussions and counseling may continue after the group session is officially closed.

3. Stimulate discussion during the class meeting. Encourage everyone to participate by asking questions, answering questions, sharing views, and giving testimonies.

4. If possible, reproduce on a chalkboard or poster paper the major charts and diagrams of the manual. An overhead projector is especially valuable for this. Discussions can be kept from aimless wandering by periodic reference to the context represented in chart form in full view of everyone.

5. Be sure all members of the group are using the same version of the Bible. In this manual, the references to the Bible text are from the King James (KJV) unless otherwise indicated.

6. Help the members choose the right kinds of extra aids for Bible study. Here is a list of five basic sources[2]: a Bible dictionary or encyclopedia, a modern version (such as the *New American Standard Bible*) and a modern paraphrase (such as *The Living Bible*), an exhaustive concordance, a commentary, and a book on word studies.

7. Devote the last part of your meeting to noting the spiritual lessons taught by the Bible passage. This should be the climax of the group session.

8. You are the key to the atmosphere of the class. Aim to keep it relaxed, frank, sincere, interesting, and challenging.

---

2. The bibliography at the end of this manual gives titles and authors of recommended aids.

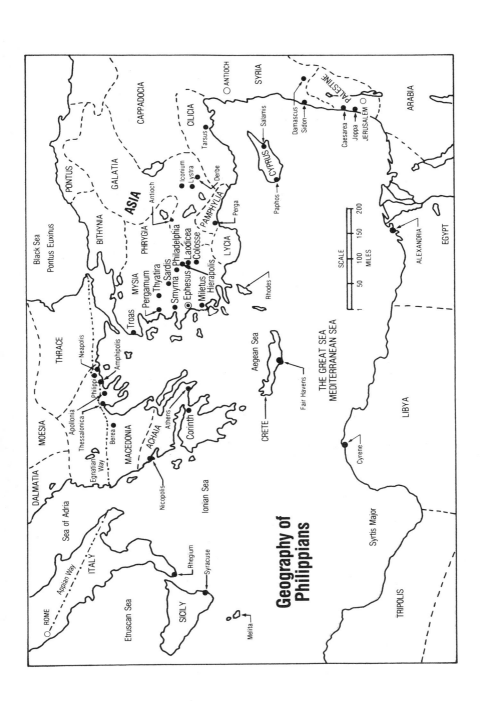

Geography of
Philippians

Lesson 1
Background of Philippians

Get to feel "at home" in the epistle to the Philippians with this background study. You will find your time had been well invested as you prepare for the following lessons in this book.

Whenever Bible references are cited in the lesson, be sure to read these in your Bible.

I. AUTHOR

Paul was the author of this epistle. He names his co-laborer Timothy (Timotheus) in the salutation of 1:1 because Timothy was with him when he wrote the letter. (Cf. Phil. 1:1; Col. 1:1; Philem. 1.)

II. DESTINATION OF THE EPISTLE

A. The City of Philippi

The opening verse of Philippians identifies its destination as a congregation of the city of Philippi. Let us first consider the city itself.

1. *Geography*. Refer to the map on page 7, which shows the geographical setting of this epistle. Observe the following:

(a) Philippi was a city of the province of Macedonia.

(b) The city was just inland (about ten miles) from the coastal town of Neapolis. (Read Acts 16:11-12, which records Paul's stop-over at Neapolis on his first visit to Philippi.)

(c) Observe that Philippi is located on a major overland route of Macedonia called the Egnatian Way. When Paul sent Epaphroditus back to Philippi from Rome (2:25), his trip no doubt was via the Appian Way through Italy (see map), followed by an eighty-mile boat trip across the Sea of Adria, then a land journey on the Egnatian Way.

(d) Observe other coastal cities that Paul visited after leaving Philippi on his second missionary journey: Amphipolis, Apollonia, Thessalonica, Berea, Athens, Corinth.

2. *Name.* In 350 B.C. the city was named Philippi, after Philip of Macedon, father of Alexander the Great. Its former name was *Krenides* (Little Fountains).

3. *Political status.* The city became a Roman colony in 42 B.C. "It was a miniature Rome . . . exempt from taxation and modeled after the capital of the world."[1] Luke recognized its popular acclaim by calling Philippi "the chief city of that part of Macedonia" (Acts 16:12).[2]

4. *Population.* Estimates range from 200,000 to 500,000 residents, as of Paul's time. Most of these were Greeks, with a smaller contingent of Jews and Romans. Read Acts 16:13 and observe where Paul held his first evangelistic meeting in the city. May this suggest that there was no synagogue (Jewish place of worship) in Philippi, since Paul usually had his first public contacts with the people in the synagogue?

One writer has described the typical citizen of Philippi thus: "The Macedonians, like the old Romans, were manly, straightforward and affectionate. They were not skeptical like the philosophers of Athens, nor voluptuous like the Greeks of Corinth."[3]

5. *Economics.* Philippi was a relatively wealthy city, known for its gold mines and exceptionally fertile soil. A reputable school of medicine was located there. It is interesting to associate this latter fact with the view held by many that Philippi was Dr. Luke's hometown.

B. The Church at Philippi

When Paul wrote Philippians, the congregation at Philippi was about ten years old. Here is a thumbnail sketch of the congregation:

1. *Origins.* The first converts were Lydia, a dealer in crimson fabrics; and the town's jailer. Read Acts 16:13-15 and 16:23-34 for the account of these conversions. Observe that the other members of the two families were also saved at this time. Luke identifies Lydia as one who "worshipped God" (Acts 16:14), which indicates that she was a proselyte to the Jewish religion when Paul first met her. The first meeting place of the new Christians at Philippi was probably the home of Lydia (cf. Acts 16:15, 40).

---

1. Robert H. Mounce, "The Epistle to the Philippians," in *The Wycliffe Bible Commentary*, p. 1319.
2. Actually Amphipolis was the capital of the district that included Philippi.
3. Quoted in J. Sidlow Baxter, *Explore the Book*, 6:181.

2. *First church of Europe.* Philippi is commonly referred to as "the birthplace of European Christianity," since the first converts of any organized missionary work in Europe were gained here. The occasion was Paul's second missionary journey of A.D. 49-52, recorded in Acts 15:36–18:22. The year of Paul's first contact at Philippi was around A.D. 50.

3. *Membership and organization.* Most of the congregation were Greeks, though the fellowship included some converted Jews. The average family was of the middle class, of moderate financial means. By the time Paul wrote the epistle, the church had an organizational structure that included the church offices of bishops (overseers) and deacons (read Phil. 1:1.)

4. *Early days.* When Paul left the new Philippian converts after his first ministry in Philippi, his companion Luke remained behind and no doubt helped in a follow-up ministry of encouraging and instructing the new Christians. Read the following passages, which support this observation:

Acts 16:10-13: Luke joins Paul's missionary party at Troas to go to Macedonia, as indicated by the repeated pronoun *we*. (Luke was the author of Acts.)

Acts 16:40; 17:1-4: Luke is not part of Paul's party that left Philippi. Conclusion: Luke must have remained behind.

Acts 20:5-6: Luke rejoins the group when Paul passes through Philippi on the last part of his third missionary journey, about six years later (A.D. 56).

III. PLACE OF WRITING AND DATE

Paul wrote Philippians from his prison quarters at Rome, around A.D. 61-62.[4] Read Acts 28:16-31 for Luke's report of those two years of imprisonment. Other New Testament epistles written about the same time were Ephesians, Colossians, and Philemon.

IV. OCCASION FOR WRITING

Paul had two main reasons for writing to the church at Philippi at this time. One was circumstantial; the other was instructional.

1. *Circumstantial.* Read the following passages and record what message Paul wanted to relay to the Philippians:
2:19-24

---

4. References to the "palace" (1:13) and "Caesar's household" (4:22) are evidence that the letter came from Rome.

2:25-30

4:2-3

4:10-19

---

2. *Instructional.* All of Paul's epistles fulfill the purposes described in 2 Timothy 3:16-17. Some of the things that the apostle wanted to share with the saints at Philippi were:

(a) encouragement to put Christ first in everyday living. It is perhaps correct to say that nowhere in the New Testament is the Christ-centered life more vividly portrayed than in this letter. Read 1:20-21 and 3:7-14.

(b) appeal to beware and to correct spiritual problems (e.g., 4:2-3)

(c) instruction in Christian doctrines (e.g., 2:6-11)

These and other purposes of the letter will be studied in detail in the lessons that follow.

V. MAIN SUBJECTS

A theme for Philippians will be developed later in survey study. Some of the main subjects that appear in the letter are:

1. joy in Christ—the words *rejoice* and *joy* appear seventeen times in the epistle

2. unity of believers in Christ—key passages are 1:27–2:18 and 4:1-9

3. keeping *above* hard circumstances of everyday life

4. growing in the Lord

5. the gospel—the word appears nine times in the letter.

VI. CHARACTERISTICS

Philippians has been called Paul's love letter to the saints at Philippi because its informal, personal style reveals so much of the apostle's character. The epistle contains less censure and more praise than does any other epistle.

Because Paul's purpose in writing was more practical than doctrinal, no detailed outline is apparent in the structure of this personal letter. However, Paul does teach about the Person and work of Christ in Philippians.

THE PLACE OF THE CHRISTOLOGICAL EPISTLES IN THE NEW TESTAMENT

CHART A

NEW TESTAMENT

HISTORY	EPISTLES						APOCALYPSE

EPISTLES: Pauline

	EARLY	LATER					General
	during missionary journeys	after arrest at Jerusalem					
		FIRST IMPRISONMENT ("prison epistles")	RELEASE	SECOND IMPRISON-MENT			
		CHRISTOLOGICAL	PASTORAL				

HISTORY

MATTHEW

MARK

LUKE

JOHN

ACTS

EARLY (during missionary journeys)

GALATIANS

1 THESSALONIANS

2 THESSALONIANS

1 CORINTHIANS

2 CORINTHIANS

ROMANS

FIRST IMPRISONMENT ("prison epistles") — CHRISTOLOGICAL

COLOSSIANS

EPHESIANS

PHILEMON

PHILIPPIANS

RELEASE — PASTORAL

1 TIMOTHY

TITUS

SECOND IMPRISONMENT

2 TIMOTHY

General

JAMES

HEBREWS

JUDE

1 PETER

2 PETER

1 JOHN

2 JOHN

3 JOHN

APOCALYPSE

REVELATION

Paul does not quote the Old Testament in his letter, and the vocabulary includes sixty-five words that are not found in any of Paul's other epistles.

VII. PLACE IN THE NEW TESTAMENT

Philippians is one of Paul's prison epistles, along with Ephesians, Colossians, and Philemon. Chart A shows its place as a Christological epistle in the New Testament canon of twenty-seven books. Note that Philippians was the last of the four prison epistles to be written.

Each of the twenty-seven books has particular functions in the volume of Scripture. Some of the purposes of Philippians have already been discussed. We will be studying these in more detail as the lessons proceed.

H. C. G. Moule has compared Philippians with other Pauline writings thus:

> Looking at the other Epistles, each with its own divine and also deeply human characteristics, we find Philippians more peaceful than Galatians, more personal and affectionate than Ephesians, less anxiously controversial than Colossians, more deliberate and symmetrical than Thessalonians, and of course larger in its applications than the personal messages to Timothy, Titus, Philemon.[5]

* * *

Review Questions

1. What made the geographical location of Philippi a strategic one?

_____

_____

2. How would you describe a typical citizen of this Macedonian city?

_____

3. What was Paul's first contact in Philippi?

_____

5. H. C. G. Moule, *Philippian Studies*, p. 5.

4. What picture do you have of the Philippian congregation when Paul wrote the epistle?

_____

_____

5. How many years had intervened between the first conversions at Philippi and the writing of the letter?

_____

6. What was Luke's interest and ministry in Philippi?

_____

7. Where was Paul when he wrote Philippians?

_____

What persecution had he experienced in Philippi on his first visit to the city?

_____

_____

_____

Relate these two observations to the keynote of *joy* in the epistle.

_____

8. What were Paul's purposes in writing Philippians?

_____

_____

9. List some of the main subjects discussed in the letter.

_____

_____

_____

_____

10. What are some distinguishing characteristics of Philippians?

_____

_____

_____

Lesson 2
Survey of Philippians

We move now to our first study of the actual text of Philippians—a survey study. Here we will be viewing the epistle as a whole, observing especially its general structure and highlights. This "skyscraper view" is an important preliminary to our ground-level tour of analysis in the lessons that follow.

Try to complete as many as you can of the study suggestions given below. If you get bogged down in any one exercise, move to the next one. The important thing here is not to tarry over details, but to keep scanning, ever moving, discovering new features of the panorama as you go along.

Survey Chart B represents the main observations one would make in an overview study of Philippians.[1] Knowing this chart thoroughly will be of much help in the analytical studies that follow.

I. A FIRST SCANNING

Read Philippians in one sitting, without tarrying over any details. After this scanning, answer the following:
What are your main impressions?

What is the general atmosphere of the letter?

Were you conscious of any organized outline as you read?

---

1. Some readers may choose to construct a survey chart of their own.

PHILIPPIANS: LIFE IN CHRIST

Chart B

A KEY VERSE 1:21

KEY WORDS:
Day of Christ
In Christ
Rejoice
Gospel
Spirit
Mind
Love
Joy
All

	TESTIMONY	EXAMPLES		EXHORTATIONS	KEY VERSES
	Christ our LIFE	Christ our PATTERN	Christ our GOAL	Christ our SUFFICIENCY	Life in Christ
	GLORIFY CHRIST (1:20)	BE LIKE CHRIST (1:27)	GAIN CHRIST (3:8)	BE CONTENT IN CHRIST (4:11)	Motives
	SUPPLY of the SPIRIT 1:19	FELLOWSHIP in the SPIRIT 2:1	WORSHIP by the SPIRIT 3:3	GRACE through the SPIRIT 4:23	Spirit
	THE CHRISTIAN LIFE—AN ABIDING JOY (2:17-18)				
	▶ REJOICE: in fellowship of saints (1:3-11). over afflictions (1:12-30).	▶ REJOICE: in the ministry for the saints (2:1-18). in fellowship of Timothy and Epaphroditus (2:19-30).	REJOICE: that your hopes are in Jesus (3:2-16). that your citizenship is in heaven (3:20).	▶ REJOICE: always over all things (4:4-9). in bounties of God's people (4:10-19).	JOY

Section dividers: 1:1 — 1:27 — 3:1 — 4:2 — 4:23

Key verses (diagonal):
- For to me to live is Christ, and to die is gain (1:21). [despite imprisonment]
- Conduct yourselves in a manner worthy of the gospel of Christ (1:27).
- Have this attitude in yourselves which was also in Christ Jesus (2:5-11).
- More than that, I count all things to be loss (3:8).
- That I may know Him, the power of His resurrection (3:10).
- Forgetting what lies behind, I press toward the goal (3:13, 14).
- Citizenship in heaven (3:20).
- Have no anxiety about anything (4:6-7).
- I have learned to be content in whatever circumstances I am (4:11).
- I can do all things (4:13).
- My God shall supply all your needs (4:19).

Did you observe any turning points in the epistle? If so, where?

_____

What strong words or phrases stand out in your mind as of this reading?

_____

_____

II. SUBSEQUENT READINGS

Now you will want to take a closer look at the text of Philippians, still staying in the survey stage. Mark paragraph divisions in your Bible according to the references shown of Chart C. (Each reference is the opening verse of a paragraph.) Then scan the epistle again, paragraph by paragraph. Choose a word or phrase out of each paragraph that identifies something of its main content, and record on Chart C. Examples are given.

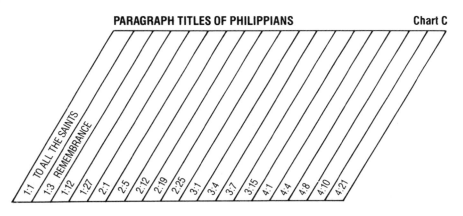

PARAGRAPH TITLES OF PHILIPPIANS   Chart C

Scan the epistle again, looking for *groups* of paragraphs with similar content. For example:

1. Which paragraphs contain mainly testimonies of Paul, regarding his experiences?

_____

2. Which paragraphs record the ministries of co-laborers of Paul?

_____

3. Which paragraphs contain warnings?

_____

4. Which paragraphs are mainly hortatory (containing exhortations and commands)?

_____

5. Which paragraphs are mainly about personal relationships between Paul and the Philippians?

_____

6. Look for other groupings.
On the basis of these groups and other individual clues, have you been able to detect any general outline of content in the epistle? (If not, move to the next exercises. Some Bible students believe there is no organized structure as such in Philippians, due in part to the letter's personal nature. Survey Chart B will suggest some general patterns that may be seen in the epistle, without forcing an outline on it.)

Write a list of key words and phrases that best represent Paul's emphases in this epistle.

_____

_____

Do the same for main subjects that the epistle treats.

_____

_____

From your study thus far, could you suggest a theme for Philippians? What about a title and a key verse for the book?

_____

_____

What is revealed about the Christians at Philippi in this epistle? (For examples see 1:5, 29-30; 4:10, 14-18; 1:27; 4:2; 3:2.)

_____

_____

_____

What may be learned about Paul from his letter?

_____

_____

Compare the opening and closing salutations of the letter.

_____

_____

III. SURVEY CHART

Survey Chart B shows something of the structure and highlights of Philippians. Observe the following:

1. A main division is made at 1:27, instead of at 2:1. Read the Bible text and note that paragraph 1:27-30 is more similar in content to 2:1-4 than it is to 1:12-26.

2. A main division is made at 4:2 instead of at 4:1.[2] Read 4:1, and observe that it serves better as a conclusion to what goes before than as an introduction to what follows.

3. The content of the epistle can be categorized under the headings of three key ideas: testimony, examples, and exhortations. Compare this with your earlier study of groups of paragraphs.

4. The four-part outlines are of a topical nature (e.g., Christ, motives in life, Spirit, joy). Each outline shows how the particular topic appears in at least one verse of each of the four segments. The subheadings that represent the title "life in Christ," are: Christ Our Life, Christ Our Pattern, Christ Our Goal, and Christ Our Sufficiency.

5. The chart shows 1:21 as a key verse. Read the verse in your Bible. One writer has commented on this verse: "This outlook on life transformed misery into melody, prisons into palaces, and Roman soldiers into souls to be won for Christ."[3] Other verses could be chosen as key verses for the epistle. Have you thought of some?

6. Compare the key words on the chart with your list.

IV. STRIKING PASSAGES

Here is a list of some passages of Philippians studied and memorized by hosts of Christians through the centuries. Read each passage and reflect on some of the stirring spiritual truths taught. This experience will whet your appetite for the good things to come in your analytical studies of the lessons that follow: 1:21-26; 2:5-11; 3:7-11; 3:12-16; 4:4-7; 4:8; 4:11-13.

* * *

---

2. The reader is no doubt aware that chapter and verse divisions were not part of the original writings but were added many centuries later.
3. John Phillips, *Exploring the Scriptures*, p. 239.

Review Questions

1. What is the prevailing tone of Philippians?

_____

_____

2. For how long had the church at Philippi been organized when Paul wrote this letter?

_____

3. Is much censure or rebuke found here?

_____

4. What circumstances were the occasion for Paul's writing the letter at this time?

_____

_____

_____

5. Identify at least two prominent spiritual messages that Paul wanted to share with his friends at Philippi.

_____

_____

_____

_____

6. Recall at least five key words of the epistle.

_____

_____

What verse was chosen in this lesson as a key verse for Philippians?

_____

7. What chapters of the epistle are identified by each of the following different kinds of content?
Testimony

_____

Examples

_____

Exhortations

_____

Lesson 3

Philippians 1:1-11

Thanksgiving and Prayer

A joyful, vibrant tone is heard right from the start of this stirring epistle to the Philippians. It is true that Paul usually begins his letters on a bright, positive note (e.g., Col. 1:1-13). But in Philippians the spirit of rejoicing lingers on to the very end. This is why one writer has called the letter "one of the fairest and dearest regions of the Book of God."

I. PREPARATION FOR STUDY

1. Read the entire first chapter to acquaint yourself with the context of the passage of this lesson. Observe among other things that Paul is moving generally from the past to the present to the future. This time outline is a general representation of the section:

PAST AND PRESENT	PRESENT	PRESENT AND FUTURE
1:3	1:12	1:18b

Try identifying a main theme for each of the three sections and record this on the outline.

2. With the help of a Bible dictionary or concordance, study Timothy and his relationship to Paul. (Timothy and Timotheus are

21

the same person in the New Testament.) Timothy assisted Paul in many ways, including secretarial work. (Compare the opening salutations of 2 Corinthians, Colossians, 1 and 2 Thessalonians, and Philemon.)

The church at Philippi knew Timothy personally, as indicated by the following:

(a) Timothy assisted Paul in founding the church (Acts 16).

(b) Timothy visited Philippi on at least two occasions prior to this letter (Acts 19:22; 20:3-4).

(c) Paul planned to send Timothy to Philippi for another visit (Phil. 2:19).

II. ANALYSIS

Segment to be analyzed: 1:1-11
Paragraph divisions: at verses 1, 3, 9

A. General Analysis

1. Mark the paragraph divisions in your Bible.
2. Before going into the paragraph analysis, read the segment and distinguish Paul's purpose in each paragraph. Then proceed to paragraph analysis and compare your answers with the titles given.

B. Paragraph Analysis

1. *Paragraph 1:1-2*: Salutation
What strikes you about Paul's identification of Timothy in this salutation?

_____

_____

What does this reveal about Paul's character?

_____

_____

How does Paul identify the Christians at Philippi?

_____

Compare "servants of Jesus Christ" and "saints in Christ Jesus." What does the word *saint* mean?

_____

Observe in a concordance how often Paul uses this title in his letters.

Note the phrase "with the bishops and deacons." Bishops were overseers, or superintendents, whereas deacons were servants, or helpers. *Today's English Version* translates the phrase of 1:1 as "leaders and helpers." Is one office more important than the other in the work of the church? Explain.

_____

_____

_____

The benediction of verse 2 appears in most of Paul's epistles. In your own words, what does the benediction say?

_____

_____

Compare your ideas with the paraphrase of this verse in The *Living Bible*.
2. *Paragraph 1:3-8*: Thanksgiving
In this opening paragraph Paul reveals his feelings concerning his relationship with the Philippian believers. Study these verses in light of the four words shown on Chart D and record your observations in the blank spaces below these words.

PAUL'S RELATIONSHIP TO THE PHILIPPIANS PHILIPPIANS 1:3-8 **Chart D**

	thanksgiving (v. 3)	joy (vv. 4-5)	confidence (v. 6)	affection (vv. 7-8)
DESCRIPTION				
REASONS				

23

Try reading verse 4 as a parenthesis, that is, as expanding the thought of verse 3. In such a reading, "every prayer" is synonymous with "every remembrance."

In what way had the Philippians shared with Paul in "fellowship in the gospel" (1:5)? (e.g., 4:10)

_____

_____

When is "the day of Jesus Christ" (1:6)?

_____

What is taught about God's work in verse 6? (Translate "perform" as "bring it to completion"—Berkeley. Cf. 2 Cor. 8:6; Gal. 3:3.)

_____

_____

Refer to a modern paraphrase for the meaning of these phrases: "it is meet for me" (1:7)

_____

"partakers of my grace" (1:7)

_____

"the bowels of Jesus Christ" (1:8)

_____

Observe the repetition of *all* and similar words in this paragraph. What does the unusual reference "my God" (1:3) tell you?

_____

_____

3. *Paragraph 1:9-11*: Prayer
Paul mentions four things here for which he interceded in behalf of the Philippian Christians. Record each one as it is given in the Bible text and write in your own words what each request involved:
1:9

_____

_____

_____

_____

1:10*a*

_____

_____

_____

1:10*b*

_____

_____

_____

1:11

_____

_____

_____

(You will want to see how these verses are represented in a modern Bible version.)
What is meant by these phrases:
"love may abound . . . in all judgment" (1:9)

_____

"approve things that are excellent" (1:10)

_____

"fruit(s) of righteousness" (1:11) (cf. Prov. 11:30; James 3:18)

_____

Paul's prayer list is short (just four things). From this we may conclude that these are top-priority needs. Think about each of the four prayers. What areas of a Christian's life are involved?

_____

What attributes appear here?

_____

_____

_____

What is the concluding phrase of the paragraph?

_____

_____

III. NOTES

1. *"Deacons"* (1:1). The word *deacon* translates *diakonos*, which primarily means servant. The other common word for servant in the New Testament is *doulos*, bondservant, slave, which Paul uses earlier in 1:1, "servants of Jesus Christ." In *diakonos* the emphasis is on the servant's work, or activity. In *doulos* the emphasis is on the servant's relationship to his master. Exodus 21:5 beautifully illustrates this relationship of a servant's total submission to his master. Read the verse.

2. *"Fellowship"* (1:5). The Greek word so translated comes from a root meaning common. Two of the ideas it expresses in the New Testament are: a communion, or association, of like-minded people (Acts. 2:42); and a contribution to a cause (e.g., 2 Cor. 8:4). Might Paul have had both meanings in view when he wrote 1:5?

3. *"Day of Jesus Christ"* (1:6). The rapture of the church will take place at this time.

4. *"Bowels"* (1:8). The metaphor represents tender affection and love. Ancient writers used this metaphor to recognize that such tender affection comes from the inward parts.

5. *"Love may abound . . . in knowledge"* (1:9). Paul's appeal is for a healthy combination of love and light. "He accordingly prays, not that warm love may cool, but that it may grow yet warmer, balanced by *knowledge* and *judgment*, or 'moral discernment.' Thus love would become not an unregulated impulse, but a guiding principle with the practical end that they may discriminate differences between moral qualities, thus choosing the best."[1]

6. *"Approve things that are excellent"* (1:10). This verse is Paul's appeal for a correct sense of true values and priorities in life. The *Amplified Bible* devotes eleven lines of text to express the shades of meaning in this important verse. Study each part:

> So that you may surely learn to sense what is vital, and approve and prize what is excellent and of real value—recognizing the highest and the best, and distinguishing the moral differences; and that you may be untainted and pure and unerring and blameless, that—with hearts sincere and certain and unsullied

1. F. Davidson, "The Epistle to the Philippians," p. 1035.

—you may [approach] the day of Christ, not stumbling nor causing others to stumble.

IV. FOR THOUGHT AND DISCUSSION

1. If you are studying in a group, discuss what it means to be a "saint in Christ" and a "servant of Christ" (1:1).

2. How can one build up a good store of pleasant memories? How will this enhance a Christian's ministry of intercession?

3. Think about the things that Christians have in common. What hinders genuine fellowship among Christians? What would Paul say today about partisanship in a local church group?

4. Why should intercession for others be a joyful experience (1:4)?

5. How vital for spiritual health is a constant attitude of praise to God?

6. Write a list of ten important spiritual lessons taught by this passage.

V. FURTHER STUDY

Study the subject of fellowship as it is taught in the New Testament. A book on word study[2] and an exhaustive concordance[3] will be most helpful.

VI. WORDS TO PONDER

For I want you always to see clearly the difference between right and wrong, and to be inwardly clean, no one being able to criticize you from now until our Lord returns (Phil. 1:10, *The Living Bible*).

---

2. A highly recommended source is W. E. Vine, *An Expository Dictionary of New Testament Words.*
3. Recommended for these studies is James Strong, *The Exhaustive Concordance of the Bible.*

Lesson 4

Philippians 1:12-26

The Advance of the Gospel

The preamble of 1:3-11 reveals how dearly Paul loved the Philippian saints. As he wrote, he was doing a lot of reminiscing—"I thank my God upon every remembrance of you" (1:3)—and he wanted to assure his brethren that he was grateful for their Christian fellowship ever since they were saved—"from the first day until now" (1:5). Paul called this a "fellowship in the gospel" (1:5). Now in the passage of this lesson he writes about "the furtherance of the gospel" (1:12), as he expresses to his readers his deep concern that the gospel continue to be broadcast to unsaved souls, to enlarge the Christian fellowship that already existed. Nothing made Paul happier than knowing that Christ was being preached. How he wanted the Philippian Christians to catch something of that excitement and joy.

I. PREPARATION

1. Keep in mind that Paul was in chains when he wrote these lines. According to Acts 28:16, a soldier was always in attendance. What opportunities for Christian witness does such a situation suggest?

2. Have paper and pencil ready to record your observations as you study this passage. This is a must for methodical Bible study.

II. ANALYSIS

Segment to be analyzed: 1:12-26
Paragraph divisions: at verses 12, 15, 18b, 21

ADVANCE OF THE GOSPEL
PHILIPPIANS 1:12-26

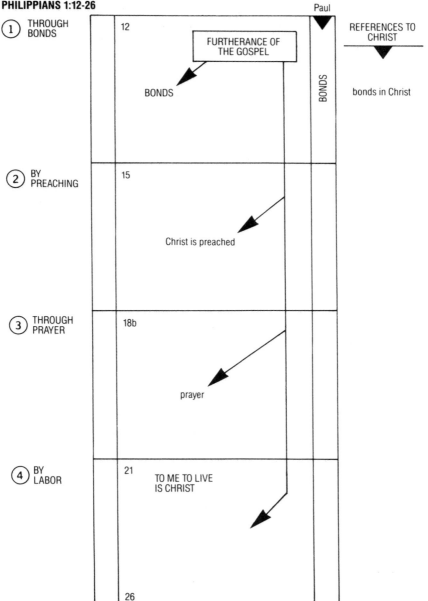

(1) THROUGH BONDS

(2) BY PREACHING

(3) THROUGH PRAYER

(4) BY LABOR

Paul

12

FURTHERANCE OF THE GOSPEL

BONDS

BONDS

15

Christ is preached

18b

prayer

21 TO ME TO LIVE IS CHRIST

26

REFERENCES TO CHRIST

bonds in Christ

A. General Analysis

1. First mark the paragraph divisions in your Bible. (The division at 1:18b is with the words "yea, and will rejoice." The *New English Bible* makes a new paragraph at this point.) Be aware of the four different paragraphs as you proceed with your analysis of the segment.

2. What is Paul's part in each paragraph? Record this in the narrow right-hand column of analytical Chart E. (An example is given.)

3. Record in the narrow left-hand column the general time reference of each paragraph: past, present, or future.

4. What is the main point of each paragraph?

5. Study the topical outline shown in the left-hand margin on Chart E with the title "Advance of the Gospel." Arrive at an outline of your own.

6. Go through the entire segment and observe every reference to Christ. Record them on the chart. (An example is given.)

B. Paragraph Analysis

1. *Paragraph 1:12-14*: Bonds
What do you think is the key phrase of this paragraph?

_____

What two good fruits came of Paul's bonds?

_____

2. *Paragraph 1:15-18a*: Preaching
Does the subject of preaching appear in every verse?

_____

What did Paul mean by the words "Some indeed preach Christ even of envy and strife"?

_____

_____

For what reason did Paul rejoice in this unfortunate situation?

_____

_____

What does this reveal about Paul's character?

_____

_____

30

3. *Paragraph 1:18b-20*: Prayer

Read verse 19 in at least one modern version that paraphrases the word *salvation*. The word is usually interpreted as deliverance, or being set free. According to verse 19, what two things would help to bring about Paul's deliverance from prison?

_____

_____

If the word *salvation* refers to the spiritual realm, what may Paul have had in mind?

_____

_____

Compare Paul's earnest hope—that Christ be magnified (v. 20)—with his great joy—that Christ was being preached (v. 18).

4. *Paragraph 1:21-26*: Labor

What do you think Paul meant by the words "For to me to live is Christ" (1:21)?

_____

_____

Verse 22 helps to explain verse 21. Try paraphrasing both verses in your own words. Then compare various modern paraphrases such as the *Living Bible*. Read also what Paul wrote in Galatians 2:20.

Compare the phrases "far better" (v. 23) and "more needful" (v. 24). Who is the beneficiary in each case?

_____

_____

According to verse 23, where does a Christian go at death?

_____

What showed Paul God's will for him at this time—whether to be kept in this world or to be taken to be with Christ in heaven? (See vv. 25-26.)

_____

_____

Read "furtherance and joy of faith" (1:25) as "joyful progress in faith." Account for the joy mentioned here.

_____

_____

III. NOTES

1. *"Furtherance"* (1:12). The Greek word means literally "a cutting before." Two pictures suggested by the metaphor are: pioneers cutting their way through the woods; or servants cutting a way before an army and so furthering its march. Paul uses this metaphor here because he is writing about obstacles that can be and are overcome.

2. *"All the palace"* (1:13). A literal translation would be "the whole praetorium." This was the imperial guard, a select group of Roman soldiers. It is not difficult to imagine how Paul's imprisonment was common knowledge among the praetorian guard, soon after the apostle began his confinement.

3. *"Some indeed preach Christ even of envy and strife"* (1:15). Robert H. Mounce writes that these antagonists were probably "a group within the church who, envious of Paul's influence (in prison or out) and stirred by a quarrelsome spirit, had increased their missionary activity with a desire to add to the annoyance of the imprisoned apostle."[1]

4. *"Spirit of Jesus Christ"* (1:19). This phrase is found only here in the New Testament. The Spirit is the Holy Spirit. Compare Romans 8:9 and Galatians 4:6. The "supply" of the Spirit is the help, or support, that He gives.

5. *"I am in a strait betwixt two"* (1:23). Literally the original text would read, "I am pressed by the two," meaning, "I am hemmed in and under pressure from both sides." Compare Luke 12:50 and Acts 18:5, where the same Greek word appears.

6. *"To depart, and to be with Christ"* (1:23). Compare 2 Corinthians 5:8. These verses clearly answer the question, "What happens to a Christian when he dies?" The Westminster church creed reads, "The souls of believers are at their death made perfect in holiness, and do immediately pass into glory; and their bodies, being still united to Christ, do rest in their graves till the resurrection."

IV. FOR THOUGHT AND DISCUSSION

1. Is Christ being preached in envy and strife by some in our day? If so, why does God permit such a ministry?

2. What strikes you about Paul's reaction to the gospel ministry of his antagonizers?

3. What does 1:19 and its context teach about prayer?

4. In what ways is Christ magnified in a Christian's body?

1. Robert H. Mounce, "The Epistle to the Philippians," p. 1322.

5. What does this passage teach about courage in witnessing for Jesus Christ?

6. How can one know the will of God? What help does the passage 1:19-26 give in answering this vital question?

7. Account for man's fear of death. Did Jesus ever weep over the death of anyone? What is the Christian's comfort as he approaches death?

V. FURTHER STUDY

With outside helps, study the subject "After death, what?" as this applies to nonbelievers and believers.[2]

VI. WORDS TO PONDER

For to me, living means opportunities for Christ, and dying—well, that's better yet! But if living will give me more opportunities to win people to Christ, then I really don't know which is best, to live or die! (Phil. 1:21-22, *The Living Bible*).

---

2. *Nave's Topical Bible* and a book on Bible doctrines are recommended in this study.

Lesson 5

Christ Our Pattern

The passage of this lesson is the first of the main body of Philippians, containing much practical counsel for Christian living. Up until now the epistle has been mainly personal—Paul sharing his feelings and experiences with the Christians at Philippi. From 1:27 to 4:9 the content is mainly practical. Then Paul concludes the epistle with additional personal notes (4:10-23).[1] This broad structure of Philippians is shown by the following outline. Note that the outline also shows which lessons are devoted to each of the three sections of Philippians.

LESSON					
3	4	5	6	7	8
1:1		1:27			4:10 4:23
MAINLY PERSONAL		MAINLY PRACTICAL			MANLY PERSONAL

The title of this lesson is "Christ Our Pattern," based on a key phrase of the passage, "Let this mind be in you which was also in Christ Jesus" (2:5).

---

1. Doctrinal teaching appears throughout the epistle, mingled with the personal and practical notes.

34

I. PREPARATION FOR STUDY

1. Review the survey Chart B to see in more detail the context of the passage you are about to study. From the chart, what things may you expect to read in this passage?

2. The names of Timothy and Epaphroditus appear in the text of this lesson. We have already been introduced to Timothy in Lesson 3. Concerning Epaphroditus, read Philippians 4:18 to learn why he had visited Paul at Rome. You may want to refer to a Bible dictionary for further information about this man.

II. ANALYSIS

Segments to be analyzed: 1:27–2:18; and 2:19-30
Paragraph divisions: at verses 1:27; 2:1, 5, 12, 19, 25

First read the entire passage 1:27–2:30. How is 2:19-30 different from 1:27–2:18, as to content?

_____

_____

_____

In this lesson we will be studying these two passages separately.

A. General Analysis: 1:27–2:18

Use Chart F to record your observations of various things appearing in this segment.

First read the four paragraphs for major impressions, underlining key words and phrases in your Bible. Then try to identify a main theme for each paragraph and record this on the chart.

Compare the four paragraphs in other ways and record these observations on the chart also. For example, which paragraph is very different from the other three?

B. Paragraph Analysis: 1:27–2:18

1. *Paragraph 1:27-30*
How does the first phrase of 1:27 introduce the general theme of 1:27–4:9? (See Notes on the word *conversation*.)

_____

_____

CHRIST OUR PATTERN PHILIPPIANS 1:27—2:18

Chart F

1:27	2:1	2:5	2:12	2:18

MAIN THEME ↑

OTHER
OBSERVATIONS ↑

What are Paul's appeals in this paragraph?

_____

_____

What is meant by the last part of verse 28 (after the word _adversaries_)?

_____

2. Paragraph 2:1-4
What is taught here about Christian love?

_____

_____

What references to Christian unity appear in these verses?

_____

What is the core (main subject, verb, object) of the long sentence of 2:1-2? Record the phrases of the sentence in the following diagram:

"IF"	CORE	"THAT"

3. Paragraph 2:5-11
This paragraph is one of the most glorious passages in the entire Bible. It is the gospel in a nutshell. It is a doctrine book in miniature, teaching a multitude of truths about the Person and work of Christ. It is a handbook of Christian living, summing up Christian behavior in one sublime, opening appeal. Spend much time meditating on this inspiring Scripture.

Who is the main subject of the paragraph?

_____

What is the practical exhortation of the opening verse?

_____

_____

Use the following translations of 2:6b-7a from the Berkeley Version:

2:6b—"did not consider His equality with God something to cling to"

2:7a—"but emptied Himself"

In the spaces below list the stages of Christ's humiliation and exaltation as they are given in these verses.

HUMILIATION   (2:6-8)   EXALTATION   (2:9-11)

Develop various studies on the basis of these two lists. For example, compare the two climactic phrases, "death of the cross" (2:8) and "Jesus Christ is Lord" (2:11).

Does this passage deny Jesus' deity while He was on earth? Of what did Jesus empty himself (2:7)?

_____

_____

Was Jesus truly human during His earthly career? Explain.

_____

_____

The last phrase of 2:8 reads literally "even a cross death." In what sense was crucifixion a deep step lower than that of death per se (2:8)?

_____

_____

Compare Deuteronomy 21:23; Hebrews 12:2; Galatians 3:13; 1 Corinthians 1:23.

4. Paragraph 2:12-18

Note the important opening word *wherefore* (v. 12). Apply the familiar maxim "When you read the word *wherefore*, see what it is *there for*." What *core* phrase of verse 12 does the preceding passage of 2:5-11 refer to? Complete the next diagram.

```
┌──────────────┐
│    2:5-11    │────────────── wherefore . . .   _____
└──────────────┘                                 _____
                                                 _____
```

Write a list of the main commands of this paragraph.

_____

_____

Observe the action words: *work out* (v. 12), *shine* (v. 15), *holding forth* (v. 16). What is the appeal in each case?

_____

_____

Compare "Work out your own salvation" (v. 12) and "It is God which worketh in you" (v. 13).

_____

_____

Does the former statement teach salvation by works? If not, what does it teach? Compare Ephesians 2:9-10.

_____

_____

_____

Note the many references to joy in verses 16-18.
What example of Paul is cited in verse 17?

_____

_____

C. Paragraph Analysis: 2:19-30

Read the two paragraphs for overall impressions. What is common to both paragraphs?

_____

_____

What is different?

_____

_____

1. Paragraph 2:19-24
What is taught here about Paul's concern for the Philippians?

_____

About Timothy's concern for them?

_____

_____

What important spiritual lessons do you learn from verses 21 and 22?

_____

_____

What does verse 24 reveal about Paul's assurance of being released from prison?

_____

_____

2. Paragraph 2:25-30
List the things you learn about Epaphroditus from this paragraph.

_____

_____

_____

_____

What important lessons about Christian service are taught here?

_____

_____

_____

The example of Christ, as described in 2:5-11, is our supreme example. How do the examples of Paul, Timothy, and Epaphroditus answer to the appeal of 2:5, "Let this mind be in you, which was also in Christ Jesus"?
Paul (2:16-18)

_____

_____

Timothy (2:19-24)

_____

_____

Epaphroditus (2:25-30)

_____

_____

III. NOTES

1. *"Let your conversation be"* (1:27) is better translated "behave as citizens" or "conduct your life." Compare Acts 23:1, where the same Greek word is translated "lived" in the King James Version.

2. *"Made himself of no reputation"* (2:7). The phrase is literally "emptied himself" (e.g., Berkeley Version). Of what did Christ empty Himself? Not of His divine nature, for the New Testament clearly teaches that Jesus was God during His life on earth. This Berkeley Version footnote answers the above question thus: "Not of His Deity, but of some marks of His divine glory that might have obscured His perfect humanity as described in vss. 7, 8." Thiessen says, "Christ merely surrendered the independent exercise of *some* of His relative or transitive attributes [e.g., omniscience].... He did not surrender the absolute or immanent attributes [e.g., holiness] in any sense."[2]

3. *"I be offered"* (2:17). Compare 2 Timothy 4:6. Marvin R. Vincent writes, "The figure is that of a sacrifice, in which the Phi-

2. Henry C. Thiessen, *Introductory Lectures in Systematic Theology* (Grand Rapids: Eerdmans, 1956), p. 296. Italics added.

lippians are the priests, offering their faith to God, and Paul's life is the libation poured out at this offering."[3]

4. *"Epaphroditus"* (2:25) means literally "charming." Mounce calls this man "one of the most attractively heroic characters of the NT."[4] The name "Timothy" (2:19) means "honoring God."

IV. FOR THOUGHT AND DISCUSSION

1. What does it mean to live a life that "becometh the gospel of Christ" (1:27)?

2. How can a Christian fulfill the appeal of 2:5? Give some examples in everyday living.

3. Do verses 2:10-11 teach that all people will eventually be saved? If not, what do they teach?

4. What is meant by the command to "work out your own salvation with fear and trembling" (2:12)? What kind of fear is this? Compare 2 Corinthians 7:15; Ephesians 6:5; Proverbs 28:14; 1 Peter 1:17.

V. FURTHER STUDY

1. Read in a Bible dictionary a description of crucifixion in Jesus' day.

2. The doctrine of the Person of Christ is a major doctrine of the New Testament. With the help of outside sources, such as a book of doctrines, study the following:

(a) the humanity of Christ: was it perfect? Did Jesus have to be *human* in order to make our salvation possible? If so, why?

(b) the deity of Christ: was Jesus truly God? Did Jesus have to be *God* in order to make our salvation possible? If so, why?

(c) Jesus as God-man: how could Jesus be truly God and truly man at the *same time*?

VI. WORDS TO PONDER

Don't just think about your own affairs, but be interested in others, too, and in what they are doing (Phil. 2:4, *The Living Bible*).

---

3. Marvin R. Vincent, *Word Studies in the New Testament*, 3:440.
4. Robert H. Mounce, "The Epistle to the Philippians," p. 1326.

Lesson 6

Philippians 3:1–4:1

Christ Our Goal

Chapter 3 is the mountain peak of Philippians, a treasure-house of golden texts to challenge and inspire Christians with high goals. A man's life can often be measured by his goals. Columbus was not content to accept the slogan *ne plus ultra* ("There is nothing beyond"). Scientists do not rest with today's boundaries of space but continually probe the vastness beyond. But the Christian's goal can never be surpassed, because it is heaven itself and fellowship with God and Christ who dwell there. Paul put it this way: "I press toward the mark for the prize of the high calling [upward call] of God in Christ Jesus" (3:14). The passage of this lesson is filled with similar inspiring testimonies and appeals.

I. PREPARATION FOR STUDY

1. Read the following passages for other testimonies of Paul about his heritage and his life before conversion: Acts 22:1-5, 19-20; 26:4-12; Romans 11:1; 2 Corinthians 11:18-22.
2. If you are not acquainted with the Jewish rite of circumcision, read the following passages for background to Philippians 3:2-3:

Genesis 17:9-14—origin of the rite. What spiritual truth did the symbolic act signify?
Leviticus 26:41; Deuteronomy 30:6; Jeremiah 9:25-26; Ezekiel 44:7—circumcision of the heart. In Philippians 3:2 Paul uses the word *concision* to refer to outward circumcision not accompanied by a spiritual change in the heart.
Galatians 5:1-15—Paul's exposition of what spiritual circumcision involves (cf. Phil. 3:3).

43

II. ANALYSIS

Segment to be analyzed: 3:1–4:1
Paragraph divisions: at verses 3:1, 4, 7, 15, 17, 20. (Be sure to mark these division points in your Bible.)

A. General Analysis

Chart G is a work sheet for recording observations as you proceed in your study of the text. Before studying the outlines already shown on the chart, read through the entire segment for overall impressions. Then reread it paragraph by paragraph, underlining key words and phrases as you read. Assign a main subject for each paragraph, and record this on the chart. Then compare your study with the outlines already shown.

Compare the opening verse (3:1) and closing verse (4:1) of this segment.

B. Paragraph Analysis

1. *Paragraph 3:1-3*
What does the word *finally* indicate as to where we have come in our study of Paul's epistle? May this word include all of the section 3:1–4:1, in view of the concluding nature of 4:1?

_____

_____

Observe that the note of joy appears again in this paragraph, as well as in the concluding verse (4:1).

What is Paul warning about in verse 2?

_____

_____

Can you explain why Paul could give this warning immediately after the brighter "rejoice in the Lord" (3:1)?

_____

On verse 3, compare Colossians 2:11-12. How do the last three phrases of verse 3 explain what Paul means by "we are the circumcision"?

_____

_____

_____

44

CHRIST OUR GOAL   PHILIPPIANS 3:1—4:1

3:1	3:4	3:7	3:15	3:17	3:20	4:1
COMMANDS	TESTIMONIES		APPEALS			
unbelief and the flesh	belief and the flesh	aspiration and goals	accountability	"earth walkers"	"heaven citizens"	

45

The phrase "have no confidence in the flesh" (3:3) may be paraphrased thus: "We are helpless to save ourselves." How does this phrase introduce the next paragraph?

_____

_____

2. *Paragraph 3:4-6*
Why does Paul give this testimony here?

_____

How did a Jew look upon each of the qualifications in the list? (See Notes.)

_____

_____

3. *Paragraph 3:7-14*
Compare 3:7 in the King James Version with a modern paraphrase of the verse.
Note every reference to Christ in this inspiring paragraph. What different truth is involved in each reference? Record this study in the appropriate column on Chart G. Observe the repeated phrase "that I may." Make a list of Paul's aspirations cited here. How is verse 14 a climax in this context?

_____

What phrase in verse 10 immediately follows "the power of his resurrection"? What is significant about this?

_____

Does verse 11 suggest a doubt in Paul's mind about his own resurrection? Compare this paraphrase: "So, whatever it takes, I will be one who lives in the fresh newness of life of those who are alive from the dead" (*The Living Bible*).
4. *Paragraph 3:15-16*
This paragraph begins the section of "Appeals" (see Chart G). What are the three exhortations ("let us")?

_____

_____

_____

What is taught about accountability by these phrases: "as many as be perfect" (3:15)—meaning "all of us who have come to spiritual maturity"; "God shall reveal even this" (3:15); "whereto we have already attained" (3:16)—meaning "that stage of spiritual experience that we have attained thus far" (F. F. Bruce's *Expanded Paraphrase*).

---

5. *Paragraph 3:17-19*
What examples are cited in this paragraph?

What is meant by "whose glory is in their shame"? (Compare a modern version reading.)

---

6. *Paragraph 3:20—4:1*
Translate "conversation" as "citizenship." How is one's "citizenship in heaven" a strong incentive for Christian conduct on earth?

How is the hope of the Lord's return an inspiration for holy living in this present life?

Observe in 4:1 the ways Paul describes his Christian friends. How is this verse an appropriate conclusion to the segment?

III. NOTES

1. *"Beware of dogs"* (3:2). A more accurate translation is, "Beware of the dogs." *Dogs* was a term of contempt when used this way. Paul did not hesitate to apply it to the antagonistic Judaizers who were making every attempt to destroy the local Christian churches. He identified them in three ways: character—"dogs"; conduct—"evil workers"; creed—"concision."

2. *"Concision"* (3:2). Paul used this word to identify the mere outward rite of circumcision without a spiritual experience.

3. *"Worship God in the spirit"* (3:3). This may be translated "worship by the Spirit of God." *Today's English Version* reads, "Worship God by his Spirit."

4. *"Tribe of Benjamin"* (3:5). Among this tribe's claims to superiority was the fact that it gave Israel its first king.

5. *"Hebrew of the Hebrews"* (3:5). Paul was a Hebrew of Hebrew parents, who retained their native tongue and customs. Paul spoke Greek, but he also spoke Hebrew fluently. (See Acts 21:40; 22:2.)

6. *"That for which also I am apprehended of Christ Jesus"* (3:12). The present tense "I am" is translated by most modern versions as a past tense "I was" (NASB*). Paul probably was thinking of his Damascus road conversion experience.

7. *"High calling"* (3:14). This could be a reference to the coming rapture of saints ("upward call"). Another interpretation sees it as a call "away from self and toward new heights of spiritual attainment."[1]

8. *"Vile body"* (3:21). A more accurate translation is "body of our humble state" (NASB). In verse 21 Paul is contrasting this humble state with Christ's "glorious body."

IV. FOR THOUGHT AND DISCUSSION

1. Someone has said, "Joy is a bird; let it fly in the open heavens, and let its music be heard of all men." Paul surely believed in spreading his joy around, so that his Christian friends might catch its spirit. Is your Christian joy spilling over to other Christians?

2. Contemplate the four noble aspirations of 3:3-11:
(a) to win Christ
(b) to be found in Christ
(c) to know Christ
(d) to attain unto the resurrection
Are these *your* daily aspirations?

3. Think more about the three phrases of 3:10 listed below. (Compare the verses cited.) Are you daily partaking of these experiences?

"power of his resurrection"—Acts 17:31; Rom. 1:4; 4:25; 8:10-11; 2 Cor. 4:4-11; 12:9

"fellowship of his sufferings"—Mark 8:35; Heb. 5:8; 2 Cor. 4:11-12

"conformable unto his death"—Gal. 2:20; 5:24; 6:14

New American Standard Bible.
1. Robert H. Mounce, "The Epistle to the Philippians," p. 1328.

4. Does 3:19 describe many people in the world today?

5. What kind of body will you have in heaven? (3:21). What kind of body did Jesus have after His resurrection?

V. FURTHER STUDY

Two subjects recommended for extended study are:

1. Justification: One of the most concise statements of this doctrine appear in 3:9.

2. Christian perfection: The word *perfect* in 3:15 may be translated *mature*. Read these other uses of the word by Paul: Romans 12:2; 1 Corinthians 2:6; 13:10; 14:20; Ephesians 4:13; Philippians 3:15; Colossians 1:28; 4:12. (Cf. Heb. 5:14)

VI. WORDS TO PONDER

"This one thing I do" (Phil. 3:13).

Philippians 4:2-9

Final Exhortations

The eight verses of this lesson are Paul's last exhortations before concluding his letter with some personal notes. Recall that Paul had written, "Finally, my brethren," a full chapter earlier (at 3:1). In the passage of this lesson the address reappears, "Finally, brethren" (at 4:8). It could well be that at 3:1 Paul was saying, in effect, "Now for some *final thoughts*;" and at 4:8, "Here is my *final thought.*"[1]

I. PREPARATION FOR STUDY

1. Review what was studied earlier about the unity of Christians in such verses as 1:27 and 2:2-4.

2. Try to visualize afresh what the congregation at Philippi was like, spiritually and socially. Were the Christians immune to such evils as friction and loose behavior?

II. ANALYSIS

Segment to be analyzed: 4:2-9
Paragraph divisions: at verses 2, 4, 8. Mark these in your Bible.

A. General Analysis

Read the short segment through as a unit, underlining key words and phrases. What is there about this passage that makes you feel you are nearing the end of the epistle?

---

1. Some commentators believe that Paul originally intended to conclude his epistle beginning at 3:1 but was led to digress for a full chapter before fulfilling that original intention.

B. Paragraph Analysis

1. *Paragraph 4:2-3*
What are the various references to *togetherness* in the paragraph?

_____

_____

_____

What problem is behind verse 2?

_____

Why do you think Paul repeats the word *beseech* here?

_____

What truths are suggested by the following:
"same mind *in the Lord*" (v. 2)

_____

"labored with me *in the gospel*" (v. 3)

_____

"names *in the book of life*" (v. 3)

_____

2. *Paragraph 4:4-7*
List the commands and exhortations of this paragraph.

_____

_____

_____

_____

Why do you think Paul repeats the command to rejoice (4:4)?

_____

What is meant by the statement "The Lord is at hand" (v. 5)? (Cf. 1 Cor. 16:22.)

_____

_____

Why does Paul make this statement here?

_____

What do you learn about prayer from verse 6?

_____

How is the promise of verse 7 an outcome of effectual prayer?

_____

_____

3. Paragraph 4:8-9
What is the *command* word of verse 8?

_____

List the virtues cited in verse 8 and next to each one record an example in everyday living that would illustrate it.

Virtue	Example
_____	_____
_____	_____
_____	_____
_____	_____
_____	_____
_____	_____
_____	_____
_____	_____

What is the command word of verse 9? (Translate *do* as "keep on practicing.")

_____

Compare this with *think* of verse 8. Is something different meant by each of the four verbs of verse 9, namely, *learned, received, heard, seen*? What is the concluding statement of verse 9?

_____

Compare this with verse 7. How appropriate is 4:9 as a conclusion to the main body of Philippians?

_____

_____